Dear ____________________

I wrote a book about you.
But you know how awkward I am with expressing my love, so I'm sharing my feelings in my own way. You know what they say, friends that roast each other stay together.
And hence, welcome to your ROAST!

Your Forever Enemy,

____

Monkeys look cooler than you when they...

I was never good at math but I know that...

Y O U +
=

Test results have come out and you have tested positive for...

only God can save you
last stage

POST A SCREENSHOT OF OUR LAST CHAT ONLINE OR...
she dies!
meow

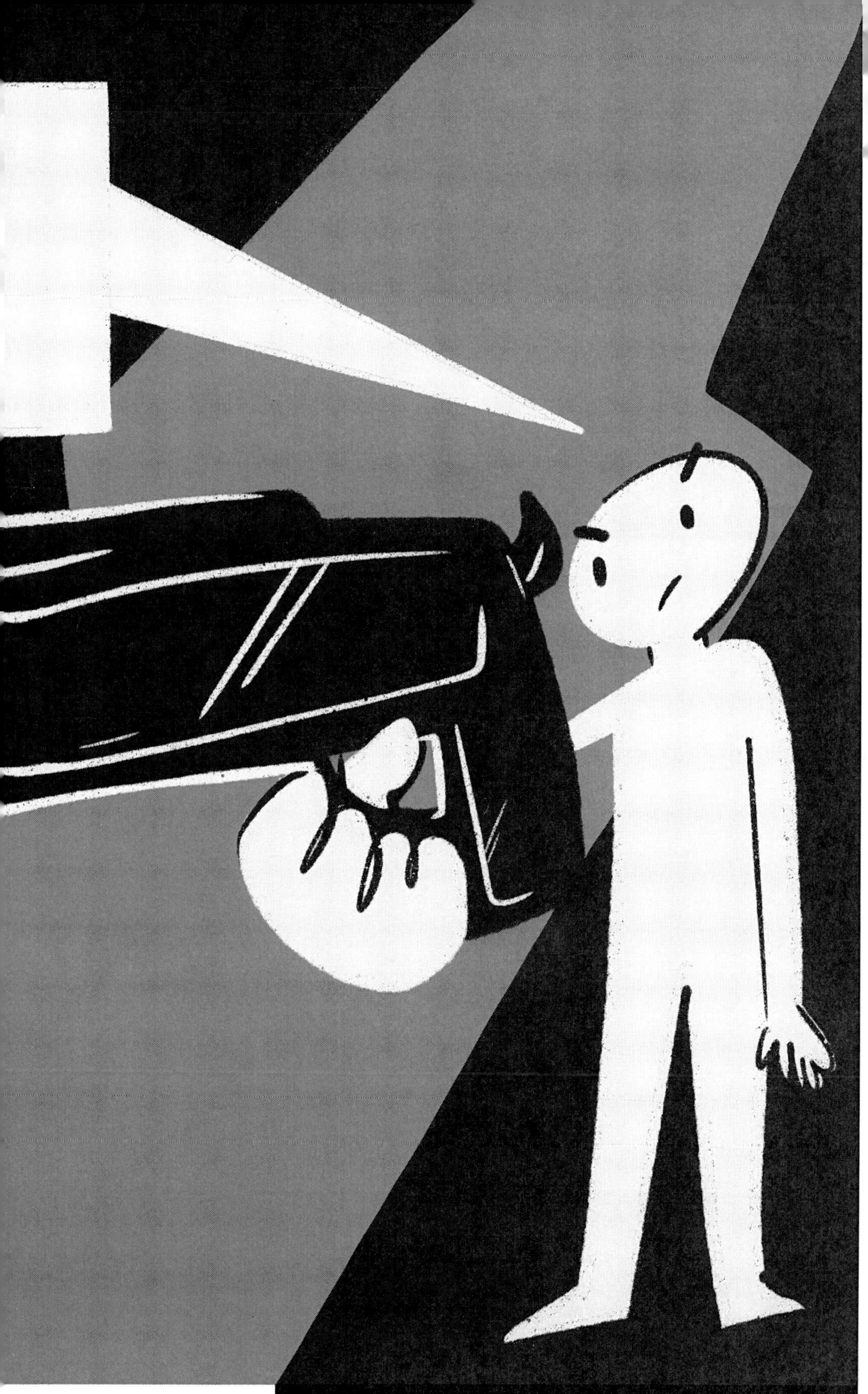

The title
of your
sex tape
would be...

write here

In older times, people were fed to rats as torture. I will choose that, rather than ...
...with you.

your
perfectly
white sneakers

I DARE YOU TO
POST A PICTURE
OF THE NEXT
PAGE ON INSTAGRAM,
OR ELSE...

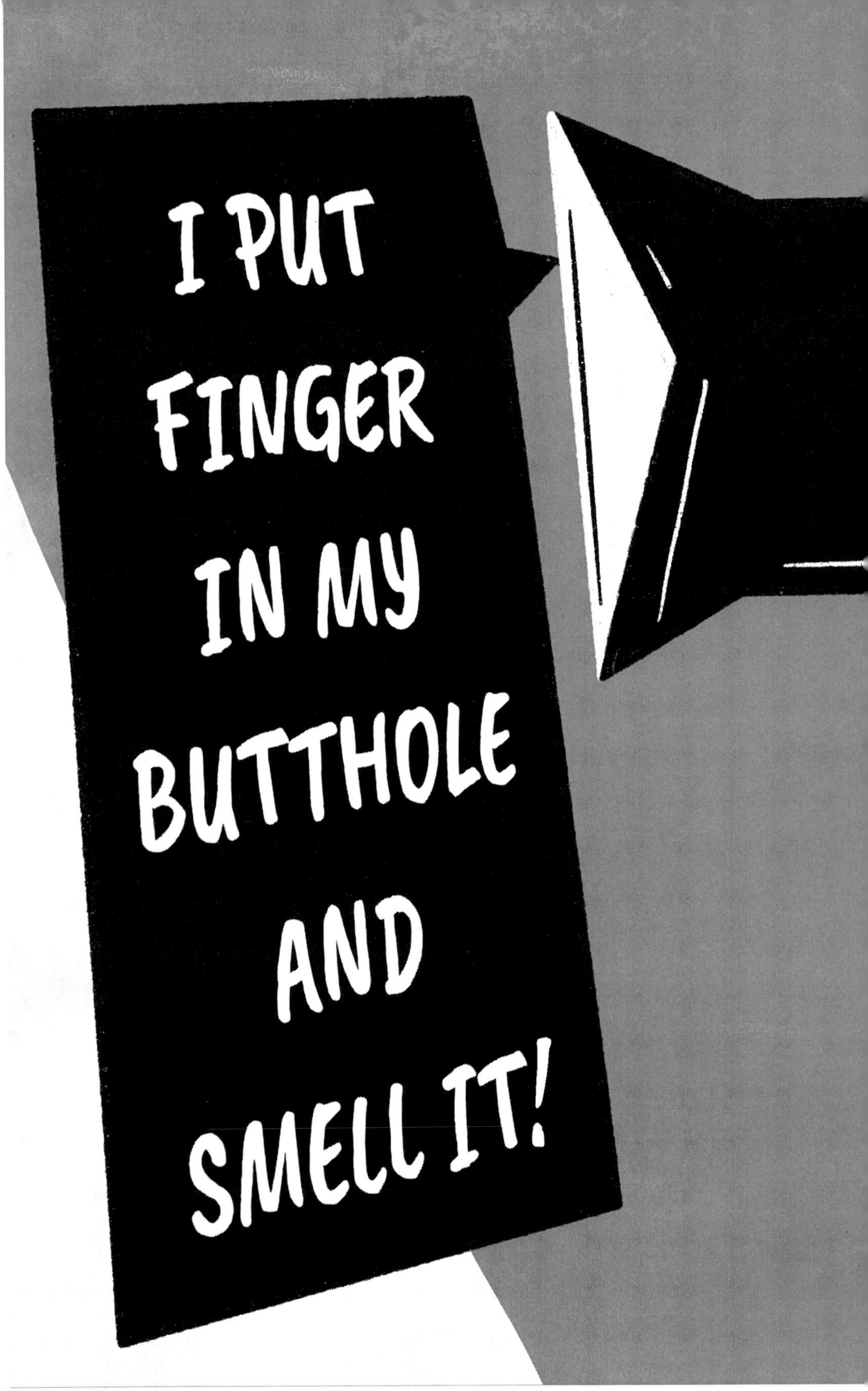
I PUT FINGER IN MY BUTTHOLE AND SMELL IT!

I wish you looked at me like you look at

I think you should hide. I heard they are coming for people with...

write here

The title of your autobiography will be

customise!

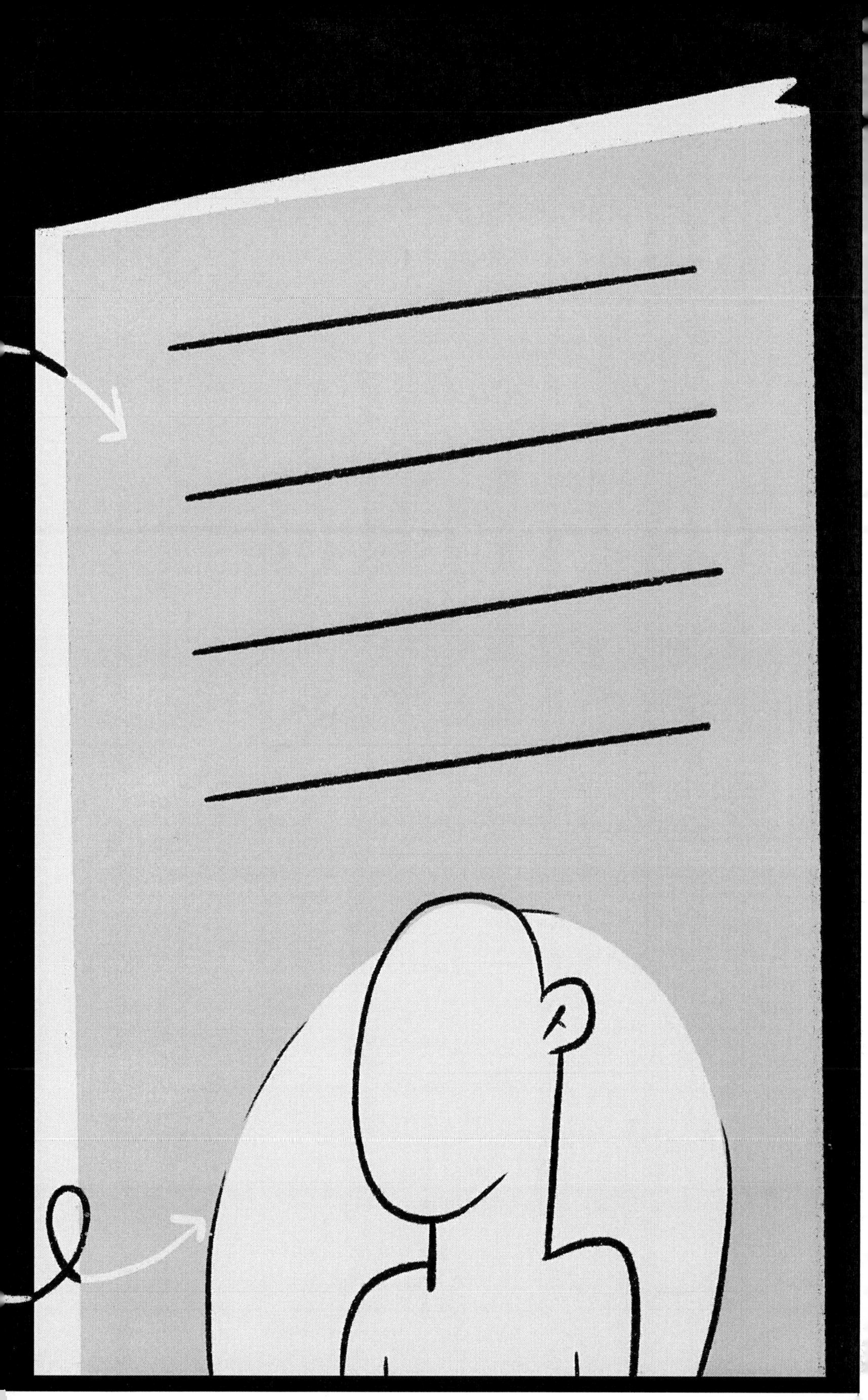

If you were a therapist, you will just tell everyone to

I once saw someone die. They looked more composed than the time when you...

If you were
a teacher,
your
students
would be
experts in

If I could travel back in time,

I'd travel
to the day
when we...

If they dedicated a street to our love, it'd be called

69 km

Your

Report Card

☆ OR ★

Cut Colour

SARCASM ☆☆☆☆☆

ONLINE STALKING ☆☆☆☆☆

SENSE OF HUMOUR ☆☆☆☆☆

DRESSING SENSE ☆☆☆☆☆

If you'd have a Guinness World Record in your name, it'd be for

GUINNESS WORLD RECORDS
CERTIFICATE

If you were a YouTuber, your videos would be about ____________

____

____

____

________________________________.

1M

The theme
for your

birthday party would be

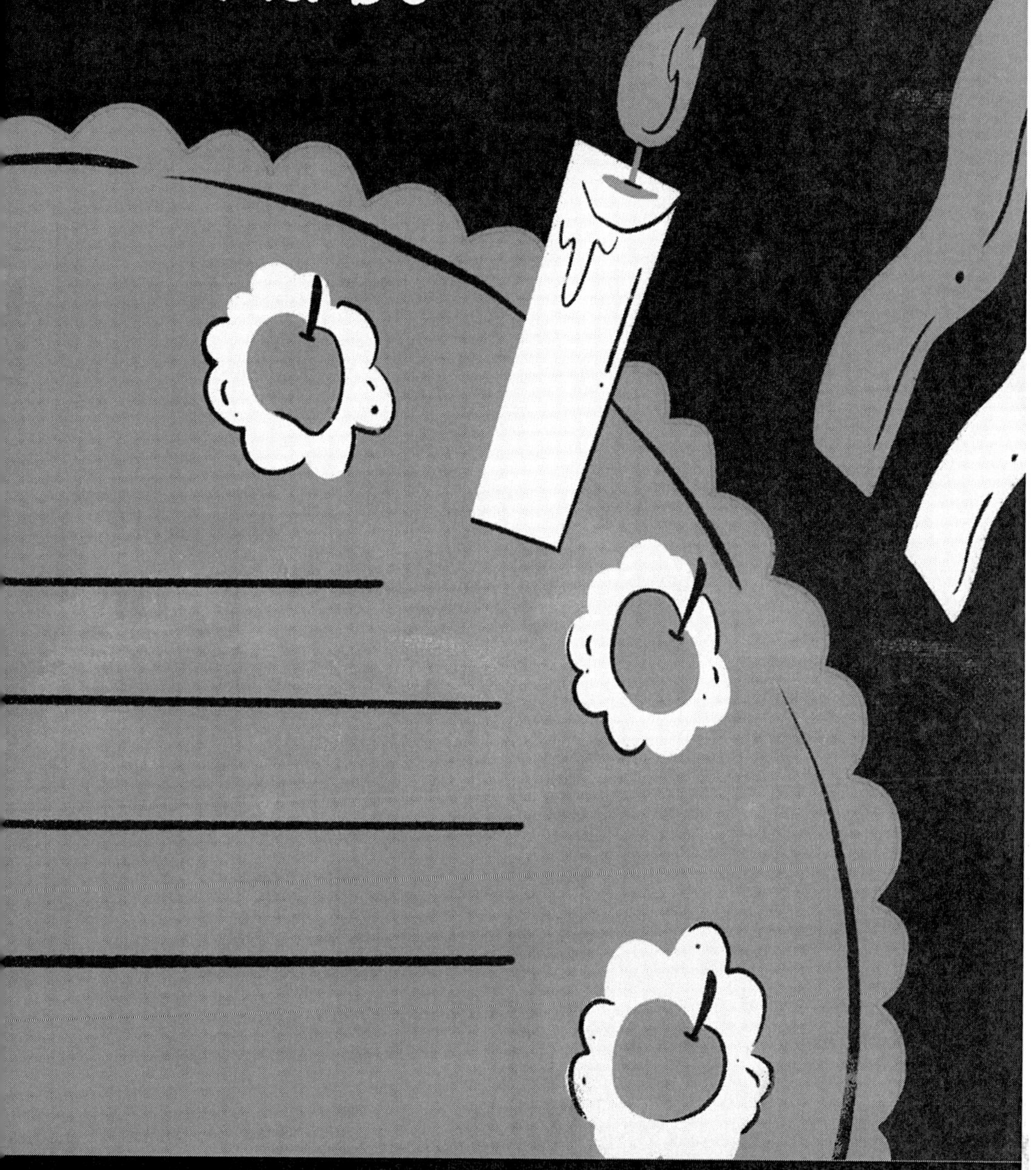

Looks like you dropped the card of your favourite club!

CLUB
NAME:
AGE:
GENDER: CLOWN/ALIEN/MONKEY
OCCUPATION:

Results of the online quiz you took on ____________ have come out.

You have received the grade:

~ choose one ~
How can someone have such a low IQ?!
Worst candidate ever
We are ashamed that you even thought of participating

@ ____________

Posts Followers Following

____ ____ ____

Bio

____

____

If someone saw your Insta profile they would think you are

customize!

____

____

____

____

________________________.

I made a
bouquet of all

the dumb things that you do

The Zoo of

____

____

called. They want you back.

you

They say, 'if you want to know someone, travel with them.' But if someone travelled with you...
you

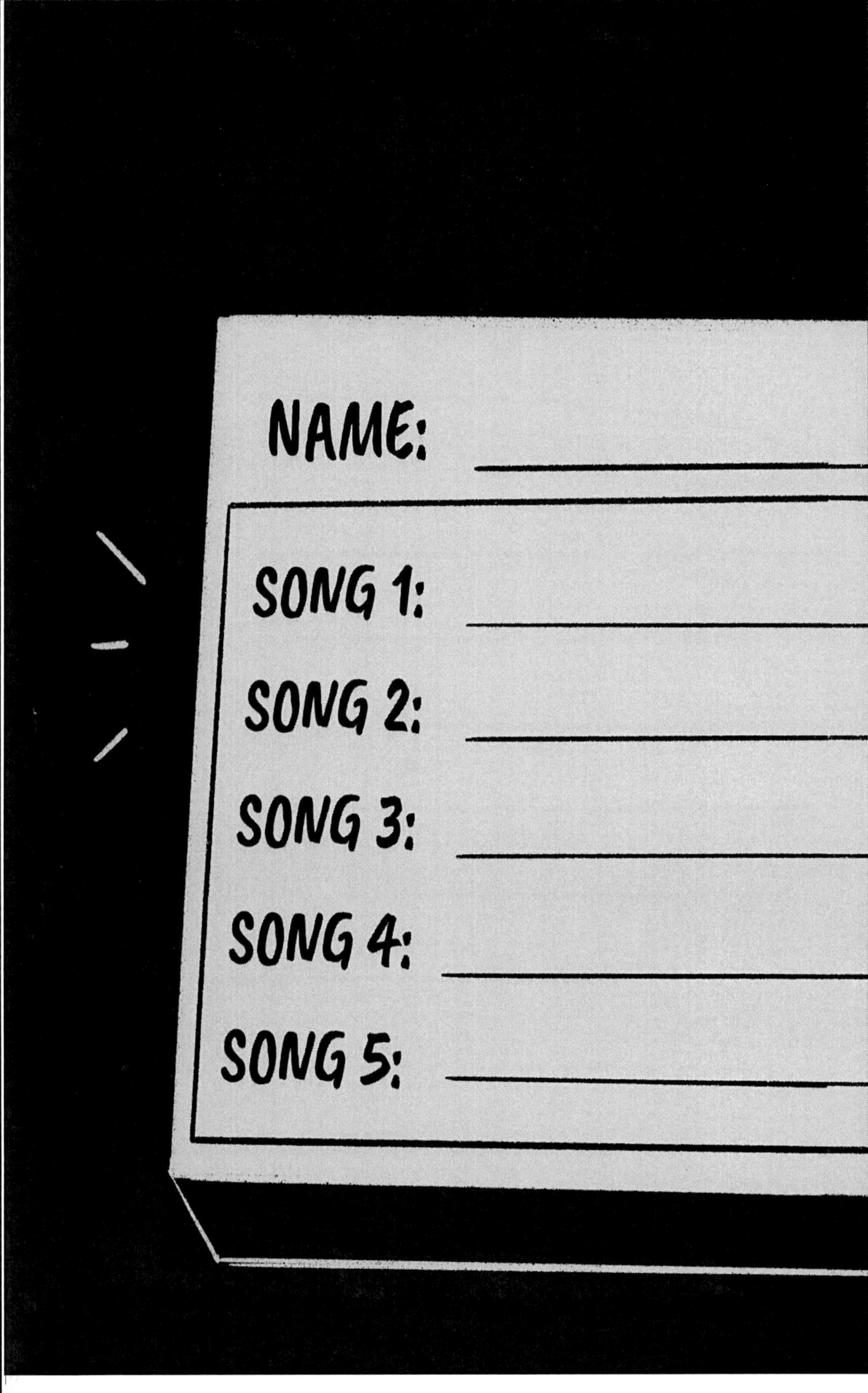
NAME:
SONG 1:
SONG 2:
SONG 3:
SONG 4:
SONG 5:

Here, I made a mixtape for you!

If you started a cult, its philosophy would be...

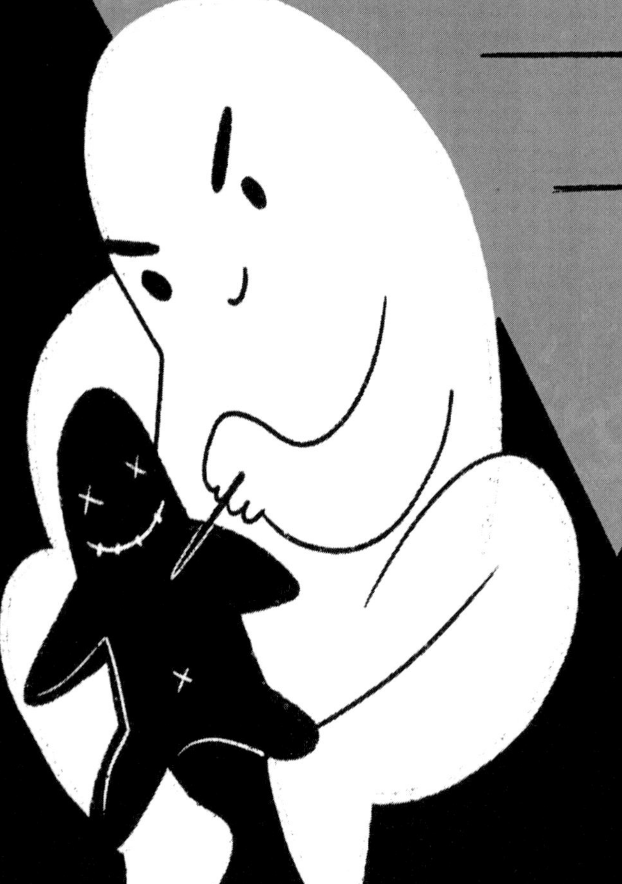

IF YOU WERE A SANDWICH

IF YOU WERE A SANDWICH.

____

____

____

____

____

If getting ready on time was an Olympic sport, you would win

____

____

medal

4

…

∞

If you'd go to prison, it'd be for

I could write you a thousand roasts, and they still could not express how madly I love you. We shall stay like this, till the end of the world.

XOXO